## Acknowledgements:
Cover photo for Barney and Jim by Mary Hansen
Layout and cover design by Gregory Hetherington

## Special Thanks to:
Martha Henry, a.k.a. "The Canadian Cleaners" for comments and suggestions
And, of course, Editor Nancy, for punctuation, grammar, and encouragement You all help make it happen!

"This is a work of fiction. Any similarity to real places is purely coincidental."

Other books by Dallas Ford Lincoln

**Sawmill Santa**
**Eagle Feather and Louise**
**Eagle Feather Boy Chief**
**Gladys  The Tamarack Goose**
**Gladys Returns**
**Big Jim and The Tamarack Queen**
**The Scout Cabin**
**The Pickle Docks**
**The Monaco Don**

for

# Mister McSorley's Mission

### By Dallas Ford Lincoln

Dallas Ford Lincoln
– 2018

Eldon McSorley was one of the oldest persons in Lakeville. Eldon didn't exactly know how old he was because you see Eldon was found in a basket wrapped in a tattered little blanket on the doorstep of the Church of St. Francis one Christmas Eve a long time ago. Eldon was adopted by a childless couple in the parish and grew up having a pretty normal childhood. Oh, he got into a little mischief now and again, but never caused any harm. His adoptive parents owned the corner grocery store in town and were considered quite well off financially for those times. They even set aside enough money to send him to a one year course at Ferris Institute where he studied business and finance. While there, Eldon fell in love with a pretty young lady from Morley and a year later they were married. But that was many, many years ago. There's more to the story.

Upon graduation from the business college, Eldon went to work at the family owned store. Both his adoptive parents had died by the time he reached his middle forties, making him the owner of the business and their stately Victorian home at the end of Second Street. His wife also worked at the store but unfortunately, they could never have children of their own. Sadly, she became ill one terrible wintry January and died, leaving Eldon all alone. A larger, more modern supermarket opened up on the outskirts of town and most of his customers began to do their shopping there. Once happy and content living and working in the friendly little village of Lakeville, Eldon soon became depressed and lost all interest in his quaint, but out-of-date corner grocery.

It wasn't long before Eldon's business failed completely and when the owner of the coffee shop next door wanted to expand, Eldon sold him the building. As much as he hated the idea, Eldon accepted a position as stocker and carry-out at his competitor's thriving business.

Seeing his old customers come and go there not only embarrassed him, but greatly added to his depressed state.

While working at a dead-end job for his competitor, Eldon's physical appearance began to change along with his attitude about life. When he owned his own store Eldon was never seen without a fresh shirt and tie covered by a starched white butcher's apron. Now his clothes were wrinkled and soiled. Some weeks he wore the same clothing every day. Customers began to complain and after several reprimands with no change in his appearance or attitude, there came a time when Eldon's manager had to let him go. He existed for awhile on the money he got from the sale of the store building and doing odd jobs for his elderly neighbors. Many days Eldon never left his once stately old house on Second Street that was rapidly beginning to show a lack of maintenance. First roofing and plumbing issues were ignored. Then the masonry steps at the front entrance cracked and began to crumble. One of the hand rails was missing and several of the wooden shutters hung askew and were badly in need of paint. The once Victorian showplace was now fast becoming the town's eyesore. Letters from the town council threatening legal action went unanswered. To be frank, it began to look like something like the old mansion in the movie, "Psycho."

Years passed and sometimes, when the weather was fair, Eldon found amusement feeding the geese down by the lake at the village park. Late into fall he would sit on a bench there for hours, staring out at a lake now devoid of the geese that had long since moved on. Eldon wished he could go with them to wherever Canadian geese go when snow begins to fly and thin layers of ice encase the lake as if sending it into deep hibernation for a long cold winter.

# Chapter 2

One sunny fall afternoon a group of children from the local elementary school came to the park with their teacher for an outing. Lagging behind was a young boy who was typically ignored by the more popular kids. The boy spotted an old man in a heavy woolen top coat and rumpled fedora-type hat sitting on a bench with his back turned away from the noisy children who were exploring the park's playground equipment and just happy to be out-of-doors.

"What's your name, mister?" inquired the young boy of the old man who was hard of hearing and had apparently nodded off. "Are you okay, mister?" asked the boy giving the old man's coat sleeve a gentle tug.

Eldon was startled awake and for a moment was unable to think where he was. The young boy sat down beside the old man and said, "Hi. My name is Adam. What's your name?"

Still somewhat confused, the old man straightened himself up and looked around, then down at the young boy by his side.

"Did I scare ya, mister? I didn't mean to. I'm Adam. We got to come to the park today from school. The other kids don't like me much. I'll bet you got lots of friends, huh?"

Eldon was unaccustomed to being confronted by anyone in the park, let alone a child.

"Hey. I got some gum. Would ya like a stick? They don't let us have it in school, but I guess its okay here. Want some?"

Still somewhat confused, Eldon looked at the chewing gum he was being offered then stood and without a word to the young boy, adjusted his coat collar and walked away. As he did, the young boy's teacher motioned for him to come join the others.

"Who was that man?" the young boy asked his teacher.

"That's old Mr. McSorley. He's the one that lives in that scary looking house at the end of Second Street. He's kind of strange. You probably shouldn't bother him."

"He didn't seem strange to me. I just think he's lonely. I'll bet he's probably a very nice person."

"Well, just the same, I suggest you stay away from people like that. Now come with me. It's time to join the others."

Eldon left the park for the short walk home. The sun had disappeared behind some storm clouds over the lake and, since it was late October, he knew it soon would be dark. He would need to light the fireplace in the parlor to take the chill off his drafty old house that evening. Walking home he found that he couldn't get the young boy out of his thoughts. Was it because the boy reminded him so much of himself at that age? He wished now that he would have asked him more about who he was. He thought to himself, "Old men on park benches talking to young children? That could be trouble these days. Probably a good thing I left when I did." Yet, there was something about this lad that troubled Eldon.

The next afternoon turned out to be just as pleasant, prompting Eldon to walk back to the park. As usual, there was no one there but a pair of squirrels hastily burying some pine cone nuts near the picnic pavilion. He wished that there were still band concerts held there this time of year. Taking a seat on his favorite park bench his thoughts once again returned to the encounter with the young boy the previous day. He seemed to recall that he called himself Adam. No last name just...Adam. Except for a noisy sea gull across the lake that was very upset about something, it was a very peaceful fall day. The afternoon sun began to warm his back through the worn old woolen overcoat and Eldon nodded off once more.

# Chapter 3

A few days passed and one morning, just as the sun was coming up, Eldon decided to take an early walk downtown. This was quite unusual because one thing Eldon never did was walk downtown, especially to the local coffee shop that once was *his* store. He had so many memories connected to the once thriving business district. Some good memories to be sure but…also many sad ones. Well, for some reason it sounded like a good idea to go there that day. He reckoned that by going early it was not likely that he would run into many town folks that he knew. You see, by now Eldon had become almost a hermit and, what with his shaggy gray beard and unkempt appearance, most people who once knew him wouldn't recognize him anyway.

Eldon dressed, put on his old overcoat, pulled his rumpled hat low on his forehead and began walking towards the old business district. The temperature was just about at the freezing mark but the warmth from the sun coming up gave him reason to believe that this year's winter would be pushed back yet another day.

The first thing Eldon noticed was a group of robins in Mrs. Jorgensen's yard across the street. Rubbing his chin he wondered why robins were still here this time of year. Global warming was being talked about lately and maybe this had something to do with that. Thinking back, Eldon recalled an unusually warm winter Christmas-time as a child when he wished for snow to try out his new sled and hoped that the lake would finally freeze over for ice skating. As he walked on, now within sight of the lake, he wondered for just a moment if he could still skate. Remembering this childhood memory brought an unseen smile beneath his whiskers.

Except for several pick-up trucks parked at the coffee shop, the village main street was empty. The few shops still in business wouldn't be opening much before nine o'clock. Eldon stood just outside the restaurant's front door looking up and down the street at the empty storefronts that now outnumbered those still trying to hang on. Every one brought back memories. He recalled the names and faces of the long since departed owners. The street lined with cars and the sidewalks full of shoppers. What wonderful smells and aromas! Oiled leather harnesses at the feed store; pop corn at the movie theater; hamburgers on the grill at the Dairy Bar; new denim overalls at the general store and the drug store's distinct antiseptic odor blended with the sweetness of the perfume counter. He was amazed how just looking at those old storefronts could evoke so many senses. Eldon was suddenly jolted out of his daydream when the coffee shop's front door swung open. A young man wearing a John Deere cap leaving the coffee shop held the door open and beckoned for Eldon to enter. Now it was the smell of fresh brewed coffee that became the lure tempting Eldon and he quickly stepped inside. It took a moment for his eyes to adjust to the dimly lit room and the greasy smoke from the grill. Eldon quickly seated himself in a booth away from the front door and the lunch counter. What delicious smells filled the place...pancakes, sausage, fried eggs, and fresh brewed coffee. Three people were seated on stools at the counter, none of whom Eldon recognized and, except for the cook and a waitress, the little village coffee shop was virtually empty.

Eldon laid his coat and hat on the seat next to him and discovered a coffee stained remnant of last week's weekly newspaper. Picking it up he was surprised to find a picture on the front page that looked like the young boy he had recently met in the park. Eldon had just started to read the article when the waitress approached his booth with a pot of coffee in one hand and a cup in the other. Without asking if he wanted coffee she wished him a "good morning" followed by a "what'l ya have, mister?" Eldon requested two plain doughnuts and some cream to go with the coffee, and proceeded to look back at the picture of the young boy from the park.

The article went on to say that young Adam O'Berry, age eight, had been injured while on an outing with his class at the local village park when one of the bigger boys allegedly caused him to fall off the top of the 15 foot slide. He was rushed to the local emergency room and later transferred to a hospital in Grand Rapids. His injuries were described as possible broken bones and a head injury. The doctor there was quoted as saying that his condition remained stable, but guarded. The article also noted that a fund has been set-up at the local bank to aid with Adam's medical expenses. Eldon realized that this was in fact the young boy he had met in the park. It must have happened right after he had left that day. The waitress arrived with his order and Eldon asked her if she knew the boy in the story and what time the elementary school would be open. She said she didn't know the boy, but school would start in about an hour.

## Chapter 4

Eldon finished his breakfast after a refill of coffee and left the restaurant walking in the direction of the school. He was surprised to find the old high school building was now the middle school and right where the old playground used to be was the newer looking elementary building. Assuming this would be Adam's school he went in and was greeted by a lady seated at a desk near the entrance. Eldon inquired if this was where Adam O'Berry went to school. The lady wanted to know if he was a relative. Eldon said that he was not, but that they were friends. The lady at the desk picked up her phone, pushed a red button and advised the listener that someone was asking about Adam in the lobby. She told Eldon to have a seat and the school principal would see him shortly.

Eldon, feeling very uncomfortable, took a seat wondering if he should have come. Just then a bell rang and the building halls were suddenly filled with the sounds of bustling noisy students. As he strained to see if he might catch a glimpse of Adam, someone tapped him on the shoulder asking, "May I help you?"

The name tag read, "Mr. Blanding, Principal." Eldon nervously explained that he had just read about

Adam's accident in last's week's paper and had come to inquire about his condition. The principal thanked him for his concerns, but was unable to give out any information unless he was a relative. However, he did give Eldon the name of Adams' grandmother, explaining that Adam lived with her in a "somewhat older" mobile home down by the old train depot. Eldon thanked him and left the school wondering if he shouldn't forget the idea and just go home, turn up the furnace, and prepare to spend another day in that lonely, drafty old house. The once sunny beginning of a new day had now turned cloudy and gray. Eldon turned up the collar of his coat, stuffed his hands in the pockets and began walking toward home.

# Chapter 5

Adam's grandmother, Dorothy, was actually his great grandmother. A tiny, but spry and wiry sort, she was fast approaching her ninetieth birthday. She was in good health for her age, but far too old to be in charge of an eight year old boy. She simply had no choice. It seems that she, Adam and her daughter, Adam's grandmother, were all living together in an ancient mobile home opposite the old railroad tracks. Adam's grandmother had worked at a nearby plant that manufactured refrigeration equipment and was the sole bread winner of the household. Unfortunately, she had recently passed away as the result of an accident at the plant, leaving just the two of them to get by on a little social security and the mercy of welfare.

Eldon walked home through wind-blown snow flurries that morning. He had decided to forget trying to locate his young friend as it would probably just cause problems. The old house seemed cold and damp. Eldon shuddered as he turned up the little space heater in the kitchen. "No sense heating the whole house," he thought to himself. Eldon put the teakettle on and heated up a can of tomato soup. Next he turned on the little television set on the kitchen counter to catch the twelve o'clock news and ate most of the soup along with some saltine crackers.

Then, as was his custom, he took a nap under a blanket on the well- worn couch in his living room.

Since the house was usually dark even during the day, Eldon wasn't sure of the time when he awoke. Looking at his watch he discovered he had slept for nearly three hours. School would be letting out and perhaps if he walked towards Adam's part of town he might run into him. That is, if he *was* back in school.

## Chapter 6

Eldon added a scarf and gloves to his winter attire and headed back to the other side of town. About half way there he began to meet youngsters happily chatting and walking in the opposite direction. Realizing that school must have let out for the day he began to walk a little faster. Perhaps by chance he would run into Adam.

In the business district there were now many parked cars and people moving in all directions. A few more blocks and he would be near the old train station. With the wind at his back it made the walk a little easier and soon he stood before the old depot which had been converted into a gardening center that was closed for the season. Eldon found it increasingly harder to remember when those huge black locomotives had come to town. Pausing for a moment he fondly remembered the sound of the locomotive's bell ringing as smoke belched from the huffing engine pulling gondola-type cars loaded with coal. "How long had it been since trains had stopped coming to Lakeville?" Eldon wondered wistfully to himself.

Crossing over the rusting tracks on the railroad bed he spied what had to be the mobile home where Adam lived. "*Somewhat older*" was a good, but understated description. A rusting old car in need of a current license plate sat in front of the detached garage that was badly in need of a new roof. Broken wooden steps led to a covered porch where two plastic lawn chairs sat covered in snow. Eldon cautiously went up to the front door and looked for a door bell. Finding none he rapped lightly and waited for a response. None was forthcoming. He knocked a little louder a second and a third time with no response. Perhaps he had the wrong house. Turning to leave he heard the sound of a door being unlocked.

"Hello. Sorry I didn't hear you sooner. We don't use this door much in the winter. Can I help you?"

It was Adam's Great-Grandmother, Dorothy, who answered the door.

"Well, I just came, I mean I wanted to see, uh…is this where…are you Mrs. O'Berry?" Eldon stammered.

Dorothy replied, "No, my name is Lawrence, Dorothy Lawrence. Why do you ask?"

Eldon explained he was looking for Adam O'Berry, the boy that he had read about in the local paper. Dorothy was not much impressed with the bearded and disheveled visitor standing on her porch, yet she invited him to come in out of the cold. Once inside Eldon said he had been trying to find out about Adam's condition and if he was still in the hospital. Eldon told her about the meeting in the park the day of Adam's accident and that he wanted to know how the young lad was doing.

Dorothy motioned for Eldon to sit down on a chair near the door. Eldon removed his hat and took a seat. Still standing, she cautiously eyed Eldon. Her stare made Eldon feel quite uncomfortable.

"I'm just a friend, I guess you could say. I only met him the day of his accident in the park and he seemed like, I don't know, like a real nice boy. Anyway, when I found out about his injuries I..."

Eldon stood up as he suddenly realized how awkward this meeting had become. "I've come at a bad time haven't I? I can come back another time. I didn't mean to intrude."

"No, no... it's okay. Please stay. I truly appreciate your concern for Adam."

Eldon, somewhat embarrassed explained, "Oh, I'm Eldon. Eldon McSorley? I live on the other side of town. You know, by the park? I like to go there and feed the geese. That's how I met Adam. He was there with his class from school that day. Tell me, is he going to be alright?"

Dorothy began to relax a bit and took a seat opposite Eldon. She was both curious and puzzled about this person now sitting in her living room. For a moment she stared silently at his bearded face then said, "I must say you do look familiar. How long have you lived in Lakeville?"

Eldon was anxious to hear more about Adam, but went on to tell Dorothy that he had lived all his life in the village and about the store he once owned and how he didn't get out of the house much these days. Dorothy seemed satisfied that her uninvited guest meant no harm and went on to explain that Adam was recovering nicely with no broken bones and hopefully he would be released from the hospital in a day or so. With that news Eldon smiled, expressed his thanks for the information, and stood to leave.

Dorothy said, "Won't you please stay awhile? Would you like a cup of tea? It will only take a minute. Please, take off your coat and I'll be right back."

"That would be nice but, I really should be going. Are you sure I'm not keeping you from something?" Eldon said as he removed his coat and sat back down.

Dorothy returned shortly and served the tea. Once seated, she began to give Eldon a bit of their family history, including the sudden death of Beatrice, Adam's grandmother. She went on to say how financially difficult it was to get by without her and now there would be the added expense of Adam's hospital bills. Eldon inquired about the work-related death of the grandmother and if there was any kind of a settlement.

"Oh, my," replied Dorothy. "That's a laugh. Between the lawyers and the court we haven't seen a dime."

Eldon asked, "What about Adam's parents?"

"Well, Adam never did have a father that I knew of."

"And his mother…?"

Dorothy stiffened saying, "We've not seen nor heard anything from her in years. She weren't no-good and let's just leave it at that."

Eldon realized that he had wandered into a part of Adam's history that was better left untold.

"Well, thanks for the tea," Eldon offered and stood to leave. "I best be getting on home. If it's okay I'll come by in a couple of days to check on Adam's progress."

Dorothy just stared strangely at Eldon for a moment then said that he would be welcome anytime. With that he bid her good-bye and began the walk back home.

During the long walk home Eldon wished he could somehow be of help to this poor woman. He found it hard to imagine that there had been no money coming from the grandmother's employer. And, surely the hospital and doctors must have some provisions for charity in cases such as Adam's, but where to begin? He silently vowed that tomorrow he would make it a point to talk to someone at the hospital and maybe get some legal advice, too.

**Chapter 7**

The next morning Eldon awoke with a purpose. Today he would see what he could do to help Adam and his great-grandmother. Rummaging through a kitchen drawer he found an old, out-of-date phone directory. He located the number of Gene Kelsey, Lakeville's only attorney. Eldon wasn't sure that he was still practicing law, but decided to give him a call, not knowing who else to contact.

A man's voice answered the phone. Eldon had expected to hear a woman's voice and asked, "Is that you, Gene?"

"This is Gene Kelsey. Who's this?"

Eldon had known Gene years ago when he still owned the grocery store. Gene was also Eldon's adoptive parent's adviser for legal advice back in the day. After a bit of small talk Gene reminded Eldon that he was basically retired. He only kept his office open to help the few remaining clients that insisted on seeing him instead of going out of town to one of the larger firms in Grand Rapids. Gene agreed to see Eldon, providing that he could come down to the office that morning.

Gene's office was located upstairs over the bank building in the middle of the downtown's declining business district. Gene was also the bank's largest shareholder and a member of the hospital board. If anyone had influence in Lakeville, it surely was Gene Kelsey. Gene listened patiently as Eldon told him of his recent concerns for Adam and his impoverished great-grandmother's seemingly hopeless financial plight. Gene said he was somewhat aware of the grandmother's accident at work, but was unaware that no settlement had been reached. He allowed that he knew the probate judge and would make a few calls. As for Adam, he knew nothing of the boy's accident, but assured Eldon that the hospital was prepared to deal with such charity cases.

Eldon thanked Gene for offering to get involved and noted that he couldn't afford to pay him.

"Nonsense," said Gene. You and your parents were loyal clients for years and I'm sure you paid me well for service and advice back then. If I can help with this situation there'll be no fee involved. I'll call the hospital right now and see to it that your young friend's bills are all taken care of, one way or the other. I promise I'll get back to you on the other matter as soon as I have any news."

"Well," thought Eldon. "That was sure worth the phone call and the walk downtown." He wondered if he should go tell Ms. Lawrence about the meeting with Gene or wait until he had more information about the settlement. Deciding to wait for a call back from Gene, Eldon wandered in to the one remaining clothing store in town, Arnold's Apparel. He had not shopped for clothes in quite a while and he was shocked at the prices. He managed to purchase a new pair of khaki slacks and a crew-neck sweater that the clerk had suggested was the latest style.

Later that day, instead of a nap, Eldon took a hot bath, shaved his shaggy, unkempt beard, and walked back downtown to Frank's Barber Shop for a haircut. Next stop…pie, coffee, and maybe a little conversation at the village restaurant.

## Chapter 8

Eldon took a seat in the same booth as before and began to scan the local paper the previous customer had left. He made a mental note to buy a subscription as he found it quite interesting.

"Why, Eldon McSorley? Is that you?" came a voice from the next booth. Looking up from the paper he was surprised to find that it was Jessie Johns, the local postmaster.

"Where have you been? Why, I haven't seen you around for quite a spell. Nice to see you again," she said.

Eldon smiled, put down the newspaper and said, "Nice to see you too, Jess. Oh, I've been around. Just don't seem to get out as much as I used to."

Not only the postmaster, but several other customers stopped by Eldon's booth as they came and left the coffee shop, mostly commenting on how they hadn't seen him for awhile and wished him well. Upon leaving the restaurant Eldon was amazed to feel a bit of his old self-confidence returning. This was turning out to be the best day he had had in a long time.

# Chapter 9

It was a day or two later that Eldon received a call from Gene Kelsey telling him of the conversation that he had had with the attorney appointed to represent Beatrice's estate. Gene went on to explain that there was no issue with the claim or that compensation was due, but the question had become, to whom?

Eldon was confused. "Isn't it pretty obvious that Adam and his great grandmother need the money?" he asked.

"Of course they do, but it's not that simple," replied Gene. There was a group life insurance policy at the grandmother's employer naming her estate as beneficiary. Then there would be some benefits from the worker's compensation insurance that the state requires employers to carry. Beatrice apparently has no known living relatives except her elderly mother and grandson. So, the court is trying to determine to whom the benefits are owed under the circumstances."

"Well, that shouldn't be too hard. There's just Adam and Great-Grandma, Dorothy, right?"

"True. But there is also the question of Adam's mother and father. Remember, Adam is a minor child, so no funds could go directly to him and would have to be held in trust until he becomes an adult."

Eldon was still confused. "From what I hear there never was a "known" father and the mother hasn't been around since Adam was born. So, why wouldn't Dorothy be the natural one to…"

"That's the hold-up," interrupted Gene. "Until the court can be certain the mother or a father cannot be located, the funds won't be dispersed."

"And if they can't be located?"

"Then the court will determine who gets the proceeds."

"But, they could use the help now. How long will that take…like a few months?

"Maybe longer," sighed Gene.

## Chapter 10

One afternoon a few days later, Eldon decided he would go back to Dorothy's house to see if Adam had come home from the hospital and how things were going for the two of them. Eldon waited until he was sure school was out just in case Adam was back attending classes. Once again Dorothy welcomed him to her home and brought him up to date on Adam's progress and the lack of news from the attorney and the court. It turned out that Adam's injuries were not as bad as originally diagnosed and he would be released from the hospital the next day. His principal at school, Mr. Blanding, had kindly volunteered to bring him home by car. She went on to say that she was terribly worried about the medical bills that would be coming. Eldon explained about the conversation he had had with Gene Kelsey.

"There may be some good news about the medical bills. I hope you don't mind, but I took the liberty of contacting an attorney friend of mine about Adam's unfortunate accident. He happens to be on the hospital board and assured me that there are provisions for charity in cases such as Adam's. You only need to let him know when the bills start arriving. I'm sure he'll be more than happy to assist you."

"But, Mr. McSorley, I just don't feel right about being a charity case. I've never had much, but always paid my own way. If we just could get some money from the court it would certainly help. They keep telling me to just be patient, but..."

"I discussed that situation with the attorney, also. I'm afraid your news about Adam's recovery is better than mine regarding the money that's owed. They attorney tells me that the holdup has to do with his mother and father."

"His mother and father? Rubbish! What's that got to do with anything? My daughter is dead and now it's just Adam and me. For cryin' out loud. There ain't no mother *or* no father. For that matter, there never has been and sure aint't none now!"

Eldon explained further about the estate as beneficiary and the fact that Adam was still a minor in the eyes of the court. He could see that she was visibly disturbed and on the verge of tears. Eldon was sorry his visit had seemed to upset Dorothy and decided it would be best if he left, but assured her he would see if there was anything else he could do. Walking home he made a silent vow to try and think of something to help them with their financial and legal problems. Just how or what remained to be seen.

# Chapter 11

The following day Mr. Blanding drove himself and Dorothy to the hospital in Grand Rapids to pick up Adam who had been there for several days recovering from his injuries. Although Dorothy had spoken both with Adam and his doctor by phone, it was a long time for a little boy to be away from home without family or friends coming to visit. Needless to say he was mighty glad to see them and know that he was finally going home.

The drive back took about an hour which gave Mr. Blanding a chance to find out a little more about what was happening with them financially. He said he knew that there would be an insurance settlement coming and wondered if there was anything he could do to help. Dorothy explained that part of the problem was the court's dilemma in trying to locate Adam's parents, Adam being a minor and all that.

Adam, who had fallen asleep in the back seat, awoke and was listening to their conversation. "What about the internet?" he asked. "My teacher says you can find people there. Isn't that true, Mr. Blanding?"

Mr. Blanding replied, "That's sometimes true, Adam, and that's a real good idea. Although, I must tell you that you most likely we will need some more information, such as a person's city or state…something more than just a name. Lots of people have the same names, you know."

"I suppose," said Adam. Thing is, I don't even know my father's name to begin with. Did you ever know his name, Grandma?"

"You needn't worry about that now, Adam. Your job is to get well and back to school," admonished Dorothy.

"Tell you what, Adam. When I get back to school tomorrow I'll check with the school librarian, Mrs. Carr. She's really good at that sort of thing and I know a little bit about computers and looking for things on the internet, too. Maybe between the two of us there is a way we can help," suggested Mr. Blanding

**Chapter 12**

After a couple of days of rest at home Adam was allowed to go back to school. His teachers were glad to have him back and promised to help him catch up without too much homework. After a week without any news,

Eldon decided to go over to the school to speak with Mr. Blanding. He was about to leave the house when the phone rang.

"Hello. This is Eldon speaking."

"Eldon? This is Mr. Blanding over at the middle school. I have some news. Our search on the internet proved to be very interesting and quite revealing. I have arranged to meet with Mrs. Lawrence when Adam gets home from school today and she asked that I invite you to attend as well. Are you available on short notice?"

"I'll be glad to come," replied Eldon. "Can you give me a few of the details about your findings?"

"I can't right now as I'm tied up in a meeting. I'll explain everything later this afternoon. I have to run. Goodbye."

Mr. Blanding sounded quite excited on the phone. Eldon sure hoped the news was good. He reckoned that he would just have to wait until later to find out.

Mr. Blanding arranged to have Adam come to his office and drove him home after school. He explained that he had news concerning Adam's family to share with his great-grandma and Mr. McSorley. Eldon was already there having tea and homemade cookies when they arrived.

After all were seated around the dining room table, including young Adam, Mr. Blanding began by saying, "Well, I have some good news and, unfortunately, some bad news for you today."

Dorothy sighed and said, "We've had so much bad news lately. I guess we should get that out of the way first."

"Between the two of us, Mrs. Carr and I spent quite a bit of time trying to locate Adam's mother and father."

Adam sat up with a smile and said, "My mother and father? Did you find them?"

"I'm sorry, Adam. There appears to be no information about your father. We obtained a copy of your birth certificate from the county clerk's office and it lists the father as "unknown."

"Oh," said Adam. "But…my mother? What about my mother?"

"Adam I'm terribly sorry, but your mother is no longer with us."

"I know she's not with us, but where is she?" cried Adam excitedly.

Dorothy, sensing the worst quietly asked, "Tell us what happened to her."

"After searching names in several counties we learned that she passed away about a year after Adam was born," replied Mr. Blanding

Eldon, who had been silent up to this point asked, "Can you give us any idea as to how she died?"

"Again, we managed to get a copy of her death certificate and it lists the cause of death as an accidental drug overdose."

All of this was a lot for an eight year old by to absorb, yet to him it was like they were talking about strangers. He knew he should be sad, but oddly… he wasn't.

After a few moments of silence Mr. Blanding announced, "And now for some good news! Gene Kelsey and I met with the Judge regarding the insurance funds that are tied up. Under the circumstances he has agreed to order them released to Dorothy and Adam. As a minor child, Adam's share will have to be placed in trust, of course. That means a formal guardian needs to be in place to conserve them for the future."

Dorothy looked at Adam then back at Mr. Blanding. "Adam's too young and I'm too old for that sort of thing. It should be someone much younger than me."

Eldon asked, "How about you, Mr. Blanding? You would certainly be capable. Couldn't you be the one?"

"I would have to have the Court's okay but, with Dorothy's consent, I would be more than happy to look after Adam's interests. It appears that there's going to be a considerable amount of money involved. First, Adam is entitled to social security benefits from his deceased mother's account. Then there is his share of the settlement from his grandmother's workers compensation claim. And, because her death was ruled accidental, the life insurance will pay double the amount insured. Adam will also receive half of those proceeds."

Dorothy was more than a bit overwhelmed with the news that she would be receiving such large sums of money. Then there were the legal matters involving Adam's welfare on top of that. She was much relieved when Mr. Blanding agreed to take on the responsibility for her. Adam simply asked if they could afford to buy him the new bicycle he had always wanted. Mr. Blanding smiled and assured him they could.

## Chapter 13

About a day or two after the meeting at Dorothy's house Eldon received a phone call from her.

"Eldon, this is Dorothy. I'm calling to see if you could come over to my house when Adam gets out school this afternoon. I have something I want to tell you and

Adam needs to hear it also. Can you come today about four o'clock?"

"Of course I can come, Dorothy. I hope it's not bad news. I'll see you at four then."

Eldon was puzzled by her somewhat mysterious call. He thought that she didn't sound stressed, but at her age he worried that it could be any number of things. Time passed slowly that day with nothing but Dorothy's call on his mind.

Adam was home from school when Eldon arrived later that afternoon. Dorothy greeted him warmly and they both sat down with Adam, who was having a snack of milk and cookies in the kitchen.

As Dorothy poured a cup of tea for Eldon he asked, "What's this news that you wanted Adam and me to hear today? If it's bad news I'm not sure I want to hear it."

Dorothy sighed and said, "Well, where shall I begin? Adam, you know that your mother abandoned you as a baby and ran away. I'm sure you must have wondered why. I think I know why, but we've never talked about it. Your mother was just a teenager when you were born and she only wanted a better life for you than she could provide."

Eldon looked at Adam and said, "That's right, Adam. I've never told you or your great-grandma here that the same thing happened to me as an infant. But, I was lucky. Some nice people adopted me and gave me not only a home, but a wonderful family. Some things do turn out for the best, which happened in my case."

Somewhat surprised Adam asked, "Gee, Mr. McSorley, you mean the very same thing happened to you? Did you know that, Grandma?"

Dorothy looked at Eldon and replied, "As a matter of fact I did know that you were left on the doorstep of the church as a baby."

It was Eldon's turn to be surprised.

Eldon smiled and asked her, "You knew about that? How did you know about that?"

"It's because I know the person who left you there that day," Dorothy replied."

Eldon exclaimed, "You knew *my* mother? What can you tell me about her?"

"I know all about her, Eldon. You see it's because...I *am* your mother."

Eldon sat stunned and speechless...not sure what she had just said to him.

Then turning to young Adam, Dorothy said, "And Adam, Mr. McSorley is your Uncle Eldon."

After a few moments a doubting Eldon began to question Dorothy. Had she always known who he was? Why did she wait so long to tell him? Why did she leave him in the first place? Should he go to her and embrace her? Why was she telling him this now? His reaction was somewhere between being elated and angry all at the same time.

"There is so much to tell. So many years have passed," said Dorothy. "Its way past time and now I need to tell you what happened. I want you to try and understand how it was back then"

Eldon, still trying to take it all in, listened with patient curiosity as Dorothy started filling details.

"You see, we were at war with Germany and Japan and many of the young men in Lakeville were being sent to fight our enemies. At that time I was madly in love with my high school sweetheart, who had graduated the year before. Come spring, and after my graduation, our plan was to elope, knowing our parents would never give us their permission to marry. Well, the week before I was to graduate, Robert, his name was Robert, received his draft notice that said he was to report immediately. The next day I skipped school and we drove to Angola and were married there by a justice of the peace."

Adam, not knowing quite what to make of all of this asked, "Where is Angola and why did you go there?"

"Angola is just over the state line, Adam. At that time you had to be 18 to get married without your parent's permission. Robert was 19 but I was only 17. In Angola the rules were different and at 17 it was okay there."

"You mean you just went ahead without telling anybody? Holy Cow!" exclaimed a wide-eyed Adam.

Dorothy continued, "That's what happened. I graduated on Friday and the next day Robert left to join the army. I never saw him again."

Then it was Eldon's turn. "You never saw him again? Did he find someone else? What happened?"

"Well, I found a job at the Five and Dime store here in town and Robert and I wrote back and forth for many weeks. Then one day I got a letter stating he was going overseas and it likely would be awhile before I would hear from him again, but I shouldn't worry. It was about that time I found out that I was pregnant with his child. A few days later I got a telegram from the war department. Robert had been killed in action. I was devastated."

"What did you do? What happened to the baby?" asked Adam.

"In those days it was a terrible disgrace to be an unwed mother and when my folks found out I was pregnant there was Hell to pay!"

"But you said you got married, right?" replied Adam."

"Yes, but I had never told my folks because I knew how upset they would be and I could hardly go out on my own at that point and I…"

"But what happened next?" asked Eldon.

"I told them about getting married in Angola and showed them my marriage certificate, but that didn't help much. My dad didn't like Robert and had tried to break us up when I was in school. Anyway, they let me stay at home until the baby was born and the day I got out of the hospital I was handed a suitcase full of my clothes and a bus ticket to Detroit. My aunt there agreed to let me live with her and become nanny for her children, but only me...*not* the baby.    Left with little choice I did move to Detroit where I met and later married Mr. Lawrence. We never had children and when he died years later I moved back to Lakeville and have lived here ever since," she explained.

"But you never tried to tell me any of this in all that time?" asked Eldon, sadly.

"Yes, I knew who you were all these years, but I was content knowing you had a loving mother and father. So you see, Eldon, I had very little choice that Christmas Eve so long ago.  All I could think of was a way to give you a chance for a home and a better life with wonderful parents.  I won't ask you to forgive me, only to try and understand why I did what I did.  I guess that's the end of my story," sighed Dorothy.

# Epilogue

Well, happily that wasn't the end of the story. Eldon insisted that Dorothy and Adam come live with him in his house that was too large for one person anyway. Dorothy received her share of several large settlements from the insurance companies, which she gave to Eldon for her keep. He accepted on the condition that some of it would be used to fix up the place, to which she had no objection. Mr. Blanding oversaw Adam's share of the funds to which he was entitled insuring that there would be enough to take care of his future college expenses. Dorothy lived to be one hundred and two, which was long enough to enjoy seeing Adam enter college.

Eldon, you wondered? Well, he enjoys volunteering mornings at Mr. Blanding's school. Yes, he still goes to the park on sunny afternoons. You'll likely find him sitting on a bench feeding the geese and squirrels, listening to the children at play, and now and then taking a short nap, allowing the sun to take its warmth and quietly disappear over the outlet at the far end of the lake.

## The End

# BARNEY AND JIM

## By Dallas Ford Lincoln

**BARNEY AND JIM**
By Dallas Ford Lincoln

# Chapter One

Barney and Jim lived and worked on a farm next to the little neighborhood church about two miles north of Lakeville. The little farm house there was painted white with starched calico curtains at the windows. The farmer who owned the place was called Charlie and his wife's name was Matilda, but everyone called her Tilly. The farm buildings consisted of a pig sty, chicken coop, granary, and a tin roofed barn with a cement silo attached. Behind the barn was a tall, metal windmill structure that pumped water into a huge metal drinking trough for the animals. The little farm was quite a noisy place; pigs in the pen, chickens and ducks running loose in the yard, and several milk cows and calves in the barn. The barn was also where Barney and Jim lived. You see, Barney and Jim were a pair of huge draft horses.

This was at a time before farmers had tractors and other motorized farm equipment. A time when draft horses were relied upon to do most of the heavy labor on the farm. Today, if you live near Amish communities, you will still see horses in use as they appear in our story. The most common breeds are Belgian, Percheron, and Clydesdales. These animals weigh between 1,400 and 2,000 pounds and are well suited to farm work such as plowing, pulling wagons, and hauling heavy loads of all kinds.

Barney and Jim were a well matched pair of Belgians. Well matched in that they pulled evenly. With some pairs there was a problem of one horse not doing its share, causing the mate to tire more easily. The lazy horse was often traded and a replacement found to take its place. Fortunately, this was not the case with Barney and Jim, which made farmer Charlie very happy. Barney and Jim were twins and were actually born on Charlie and Tilly's farm four years ago. So much alike in size and color that even Charlie couldn't tell them apart. Strange as it may seem, both horses knew their names when Charlie called them and where each was to stand while being hitched to a plow or wagon. Charlie kept them well fed and never over worked or abused them. He always made sure their stalls in the barn were clean and fresh straw bedding added each day.

It was a small farm, but a pleasant and satisfying place to live and work. Each spring Tilly planted and tended a large garden that produced all kinds of vegetables to preserve for winter. Wild huckleberries and blackberries as big as your thumb grew wild in the marshy area just across the dusty two-track road that meandered past their place. Behind the house was a tiny grove of fruit trees that produced several varieties of luscious apples and succulent pears. Each day the chickens laid an abundant supply of both white and brown eggs while the cows provided fresh milk and cream from which to make butter and cheese. A huge black wood fired range in the kitchen gave up heavenly odors of bread baking along with biscuits, juicy berry pies, fruit filled cookies, and cakes of all kinds. (Tilly's German chocolate cake won a blue ribbon at the county fair twice in a row!)

Besides all the farm animals, Charlie and Tilly had several barn cats and a beautiful collie dog named Suzy. Suzy was very intelligent and each day, late in the afternoon, she would go out to the pasture and herd the cows back home to the barn at milking time. Sadly, Charlie and Tilly had no children. The farm was such an ideal place to raise a family and many of their close neighbors had large numbers of children. It seems that Charlie and Tilly had given up hope of ever having children of their own. Tilly could often be found helping out over at a neighbor's place when a new child was born. Other times volunteering to babysit little ones in her home when their parents needed help during harvest. Sometimes she cried when the babies in her care were picked-up to go back to their homes at the end of the day. The silence in the house when the children were gone left Tilly feeling empty and sad. Charlie often found Tilly lying in bed, quietly sobbing to herself, when he came in from the field or evening chores. Sometimes it was a cold supper for Charlie with just Suzy as his companion.

One summer evening, just after he had finished milking the cows, he was pleasantly surprised to find Tilly in the kitchen wearing a freshly starched apron and a big smile. The kitchen table was covered with a new flowery tablecloth, their best china and silverware, and a lit candle with fresh flowers as the center piece. There was fried chicken on the stove, a steaming bowl of mashed potatoes, giblet gravy, fresh picked corn on the cob, and a warm mince meat pie.

"Well, my, my my," exclaimed Charlie. "What's this all about? What's the occasion?"

Tilly, who was at the stove stirring the gravy, looked over her shoulder and said, "Get out of those barn clothes and go get washed-up while I finish setting the table. Now, just go on and don't ask any questions."

"Yes, ma'am," replied Charlie. I don't know what you're up to, but I like it already."

And off he went, puzzled but pleased and drooling over the wonderful kitchen smells that now filled the whole house. Suzy sat patiently outside the kitchen's screened door now and then scratching and barking to make sure she wasn't being ignored. Tilly turned towards the door and said, "Suzy, you be a good girl and wait your turn. I want to talk to Charlie first then you can come in." Suzy gave a quizzical look to her mistress, stretched, yawned, and then laid down on the doorstep.

Well, as they say, "good things come to those who stand and wait," and Tilly had exciting news to share. Tilly had discovered that she was going to have a baby.

Charlie could hardly believe his ears. At last the one thing missing in their home would soon be in place after all these years of waiting. Life on their little farm would now be complete.

## Chapter 2

The rainfall that year had been above average and, by fall, the land produced an abundant crop. By mid-September the harvest was in full swing all around the neighborhood. In those days the neighbors would often gather at each farm, working together to help bring in the crops. With wooden planks over saw horses for tables set up out on the lawn, the farmer's wives would pile them high with food for the noontime meal. Colorful tablecloths were spread and set with tin plates and cups. Next came platters of fried pork chops, chicken, and ham; steaming bowls of boiled potatoes and vegetables; loaves of home-made bread and jars of jams; cold well water, tea and coffee to drink; pies, cake and chilled watermelon for desert. Make-shift seating often consisted of potato crates, bags of feed, and empty wooden nail kegs.

At high noon the lady of the house where the harvest was taking place would begin ringing the heavy old dinner bell that hung on a post in the yard. This was the signal that summoned the men and their sons from the fields. First the horses were watered and fed. Then the men and boys would wash-up, find a seat and partake of the mid-day feast. And feast they did! The women made sure the bowls and platters were kept full and the cups filled and re-filled time and again to satisfy the noisy, thirsty crew of harvesters. The young children impatiently tugged at their mother's aprons, pleading and asking when it would be their turn to eat.

After a meal of this size most of the men and older boys found a shady spot in the yard and took a much needed nap. Once the harvest crew was finished eating the women and children would comprise the "second shift." Dirty dishes were quickly washed, dried, and placed back on the tables. The empty bowls and platters were hurriedly refilled with the meat and vegetables that remained. This would be an opportunity for the farm ladies to eat and relax while catching up on any local gossip. The older girls would be in charge of seeing that the little ones were fed and got their naps. This was a typical day on the farm at harvest-time and would be a scene that would be repeated over and over again until each neighbor's crops were brought in and safely stored for the long winter months to follow.

## Chapter Three

The winter that followed that year was particularly long and hard. Howling winds and blinding snow blew in from the north. Roads became filled with drifting snow making them virtually impassable. Temperatures fell to zero and below for days on end. Guide ropes were tied from the houses to the barns so those tending to the animals would not become disoriented wading through waist deep snow in white-out conditions. Folks would go for days without seeing another soul. The one room school and neighborhood church were both closed "until further notice." The mail stopped and store bought supplies like sugar, flour and coffee began to run low. Tilly kept herself busy with daily cooking, cleaning and baking chores. In the evening she turned to sewing clothes for the new baby. Charlie fed the animals and did the milking twice a day. Just keeping the wood box filled with firewood was nearly a full time job. Fortunately, Charlie had put up a good wood supply that fall and was glad for that.

As good fortune would have it, both Charlie and Tilly were very healthy that winter, while many in the area suffered from flu and other types of respiratory ailments. Any type of illness could be cause for alarm, as getting to a doctor in snow-bound conditions was near impossible. The livestock fared no better than their owners under such harsh conditions. Many of the older animals would not survive until spring. Tilly was glad her baby was not due to be born until March. Hopefully, by then the snow would be gone and the roads passable once more. The days dragged on and time seemed to pass ever so slowly that winter. Rarely was there a day when the sun shone. Dark, dreary, and depressing were words that best described conditions in the neighborhood. But, over at Charlie and Tilly's place, there was growing excitement at the thoughts of a new addition to their family.

## Chapter Four

The month of March in mid-Michigan could be a harbinger of many things to come. Warm rains from the southwest hastened the thawing of snow covered fields. Buckets for catching sap for making syrup soon adorned maple trees in the groves. The animals in the barn became restless, sensing that the time was near when they would be free to once again romp in the pasture. Unfortunately, March could also be a month of strong wind storms, sleet, hail and even tornadoes. This was a time when there were no automobiles, few hospitals, and doctors made their rounds of the sick and injured by horse and buggy. Telephones in the rural communities were an unavailable luxury for most and electricity was only available in towns and cities. And just like livestock, babies were born at home on the farm.

On the first day of March that year "old man winter" gave way to sunny seventy degree weather. Warm balmy winds and a misty rain gave rise to a hint of an early spring. Perhaps spring was really just actually around the corner? Maybe the worst winter in years would now become just a memory. But no matter how harsh this year's weather, the area's old-timers insisted that it was much worse back in their day. Most weather forecasts in those days came from various farm journals and publications. The Old Farmer's Almanac reminded its subscribers that, "If March comes in like a lamb it will go out like a Lion!" As everyone would soon find out, spring was definitely not, "just around the corner."

## Chapter 5

Tilly knew that it was near time for her baby to be born. She suggested to Charlie that, as soon as the roads were passable, he should hitch up Barney and Jim and go into town for their needed grocery staples and supplies. She also reminded him to let Doctor Andersen know that he may be needed at their place in the near future. Tilly hoped at the same time that her labor would be short, but also that doctor Andersen would be able to get to the farm in time. Tilly comforted herself in knowing that with good roads and a fast buggy the trip from town would not take long. Charlie had spent much of his time lovingly building a wooden crib for the baby. She hoped that there would be time to finish the little quilt she made special for the baby's new crib. Soon they would have to pick out some names, too.

The early spring-like weather lasted but a few short days then a cold front from the north moved in. Ominous black clouds swirled in low over head rattling the windows and pelting the tin roof with sleet. Branches on the trees glistened with a freezing coat of ice. Maybe it was fear of the storm or maybe it was just time, but Tilly's baby was about to be born.

Breakfast was over and Tilly was anxiously looking out the kitchen window at the developing storm. "Charlie, I think you should fetch the doctor. I know the weather is looking bad, but it might get worse. You best go now. I think our baby wants to be born soon."

"You think the baby is coming right now? Maybe I should wait a bit and see if this all blows over," replied Charlie who was also eyeing the ugly weather outside.

"I'm sorry, but you need to go right now," urged Tilly as a strong labor pain caused her to grimace and grab hold of the table for support. Charlie realized that despite the storm he needed to go find the doctor at once. "Do you want me to bring you anything from town?" he asked as he headed out the door for the barn.

"For goodness sake, Charlie. Please, just bring me the doctor!" exclaimed an exasperated Tilly.

## Chapter 6

Once in the barn Charlie apologized to Barney and Jim as they were being hitched to the buggy. "Sorry, boys. I don't want to go either, but I'm about to become a father and we need to go get Doc Andersen bad weather or not." And off they went into driving sleet that was fast changing to what would become a wet, heavy snow. Charlie was gratefully relived to find the doctor at home as he halted the buggy near the hitching post in front of the house that also served as the doctor's office.

"My goodness, Charlie. What brings you out on a day like this? Come in by the fire and warm yourself," said doctor Andersen as he led Charlie into his office.

"Well Doc, you see I'm going to have a baby and Tilly says you're to come now and I don't know if…"

"Whoa there, Charlie. Take a breath man. Now tell me, who's having a baby?"

"It's me…ah…I mean it's us, you know, I mean it's Tilly and you are to come with me, now."

"Well that is very good news. Congratulations, my friend. Are you sure that she…"

"Oh yeah, Doc. We're…I mean Tilly's sure. That's why she sent me here."

Well, I guess she wouldn't ask the both of us out in this weather if she wasn't sure." The doctor shuddered as he looked out the window of his office and thinking, "I may be getting a little too old for this," then said aloud, "You grab my bag while I get dressed for the trip."

## Chapter 7

As luck would have it the wind and snow had let up a bit and the trip back to the farm went smoothly in spite of icy patches in the road here and there. Charlie let the doctor off at the house and took Barney and Jim to the barn realizing he had forgotten to do the milking that morning. That would have to come first and feed and clean bedding for the horses would have to come later. Sometime later, with the chores finished, Charlie hurriedly made his way back to the house as the storm began to worsen once again. He was surprised to find both the doctor and Tilly sitting at the kitchen table.

"Your lunch is still warm," said Tilly indicating a covered dish on the wood stove. I hope you don't mind. The doctor and I started without you."

"You mean you had the baby already?" said Charlie.

"Heavens no, man." laughed the good doctor. "Your baby is not coming for a while. Sit down and eat your lunch. We'll likely be at this for quite a spell. There's plenty of time for a game of checkers or two before evening chores."

As the afternoon wore on and evening approached the storm once again picked up in intensity as did Tilly's concerns and her labor. The wind buffeted the roof and rattled the windows causing everyone to feel a bit on edge. Charlie busily stoked the fire and made several trips to the barn to check on the animals that also seemed nervous as wind driven snow began seeping through the cracks in the siding of the building. Doctor Andersen kept a close watch on Tilly's progress and reassured her that things were progressing normally. Unfortunately, the storm was now progressing to blizzard-like conditions. Blowing and drifting snow was piling up everywhere. It was turning out to be the worst storm of the entire winter.

# Chapter 8

The wind up clock on the shelf in the living room chimed the twelve o'clock hour awakening Charlie who had fallen asleep with his arms folded and his head on the kitchen table. Doctor Andersen had just come from the bedroom and poured himself a cup of coffee offering the pot to Charlie.

"How's Tilly? Do we have a baby yet?" asked Charlie as he stretched and rubbed his eyes. "I guess I must have fallen asleep. What time is it?"

"It's late and I'm a little worried about Tilly in there," said the doctor gesturing towards the bedroom. "She hasn't had much rest and…"

"She's going to be alright, isn't she Doc? I mean, this takes time I know, but I remember the time one of our cows was..."

"If this goes on much longer, I'm afraid she may have to have surgery and I haven't come prepared for that."

"What are you going to do Doc?" asked Charlie suddenly becoming aware of the doctor's long face.

"Right now there's nothing more I can do except wait and see if things get a little better. Why don't you go to her for awhile and I'll catch a few winks. I'll be right here if I'm needed."

## Chapter 9

Well, things did not improve with either Tilly or the howling winds outside. It was near five in the morning and a long way from becoming light outside. Doctor Andersen insisted that Charlie go to the barn as usual to care for the animals. He knew that Tilly and the baby were in danger and that would give Charlie something to do instead of pacing in the kitchen.

"Your poor wife is about worn out and I'm about out of ideas," the doctor confided in Charlie when he returned from the barn. I need to get her to town soon."

"But Doc, you've not been outside. It's terrible! I had to follow the guide rope from the barn just now to find my way back to the house."

"Well, maybe the storm will lighten up a bit come dawn, but we haven't much time I'm afraid. See to your wife, man. I'll make some fresh coffee."

Things were not looking good for Tilly and her baby. The only good news was that with the dawn the sun came out and storm seemed to have blown itself out. Yet, the thought of travel by buggy seemed impossible. Charlie and the doctor stood looking out the kitchen window at the snow drifts. Neither man spoke. Charlie looked away with his head bowed as if in prayer.

"Did you hear that?" asked the doctor breaking the silence in the room.

Startled, Charlie started for the bedroom. "No wait...Listen...I think I can hear sleigh bells," said the doctor with an ear cocked toward the window. "Well now, would you look at that? Appears you've got company, Charlie."

Charlie glanced back at the window to see what the doctor was talking about. Company? Surely, no one could be out in this weather.

# Chapter 10

About half way between the house and barn appeared a team of horses pulling a sleigh. Coming to a stop the horses snorted and neighed expelling great clouds of their frosty breath into the crisp wintery air. Driving the team was a large hulk of a man with a snow white beard all dressed in a black with a fur trimmed coat that came down to the top of his boots. On his head he wore a heavy woolen cap pulled down over his ears while a flowing red wool scarf encircled his neck. He jumped down from the sleigh and began wading through the snow towards the house. Charlie could hardly believe his eyes. It was his neighbor and old friend, Abe Palmer, who lived about two miles east. Charlie held open the door as Abe stomped into the kitchen, removing his cap and scarf and heading straight to the wood stove without saying a word.

"What in the world brings you out in weather like this?" asked a still disbelieving Charlie.

"Well, my misses knew Tilly was due to have that baby soon and, what with this storm, she suggested I go check up on you folks." Acknowledging the doctor Abe added, " And with the Doc already here there must be some good news, I hope?"

"Oh Abe, you couldn't have come at a better time. Tilly's in a bad way and the Doc here says we need to get her to town. I can't believe you…"

The doctor interrupted saying, "Glad to see you Abe. I need to get Tilly to town at once. We don't have any time to lose. Can your team make it to Lakeville from here with all the snow?"

"I don't know," said Abe. They're pretty winded making it just this far and who knows what the road south of here is like with all the blowing and drifting last night. I'm not sure that…"

"We have to try," pleaded Charlie grabbing Abe by the arm. "We'll put your team in the barn and hitch up Barney and Jim. I'm sure they can make it from here."

"There's no time to waste. We need to go now!" insisted the doctor.

While the doctor explained to Tilly about the planned trip to town, Charlie rounded up enough warm clothes and blankets for the three of them that would be going on the sleigh. Abe agreed to switch teams and would stay behind to tend to the animals. He knew his "misses" would be worried when he didn't come home but, for at least for tonight, she and their two boys would have to be in charge at his place.

## Chapter 11

Charley and the doctor helped get Tilly loaded onto a bed of straw in the back of the sleigh. Barney and Jim were nervously pawing the snow, shuddering and eager to go. The doctor rode with Tilly, Charlie drove the team and away they went. Abe watched as the sleigh disappeared into the swirling snow as it headed toward the town some two miles to the south.  He said a silent prayer, shuddered then quickly sought the warmth of the house.

"Come on, my boys," Charlie yelled to his team. "We have to get Tilly to town as fast as we can.  I just know you can do it."

The team, being well rested, pulled the sleigh as though they realized that their mistress was in danger. Busting through chest-high drifts they steadily hauled their precious cargo stopping only to rest at the top several hills that were part of the roadway.

Tilly was in much discomfort with the rough and bumpy ride.  Her medical companion offered assurance that they were almost to town where he would safely deliver the baby.  Charlie was terribly worried about Tilly and the baby while at the same time extremely proud of the heroic efforts of Barney and Jim.

"Just help me get Tilly into the office then you can take the horses to the livery stable just down the street. They will be well taken care of," the doctor said to Charlie as they reached his house in the village.  Bernice, the doctor's wife, met them at the door and quickly got Tilly to a bed in the office.  The room was heated by an old pot bellied stove that glowed cherry red from the coal fire that burned inside.  Bernice gave her husband a worried look as he prepared to do the best he could with his pitifully outdated operating equipment.

# Chapter 12

Spring finally came to the area about mid April that year.  Soon it would be time to start planting.  The frost was out of the ground and all the snow had melted added much needed moisture to the fields.  Things were getting somewhat back to normal after the long, hard winter.  The road to town was still muddy and difficult to travel.

However, the one room school down the road was open and church services had resumed. Even the mail was being delivered occasionally.

Charlie and Abe sat out on the porch near the kitchen talking about things pertaining to spring planting and the price for wheat and corn. Suzy lay at their feet enjoying the late afternoon sunshine. From behind the kitchen's screen door came a voice.

"If you two can stop talking farming for a bit I thought you might like some coffee and homemade cinnamon rolls. I just took them out of the oven and they're still hot," offered Tilly.

Abe said, "That woman of yours is sure a good cook. I hope I can get her to send a couple of those gooey buns home with me."

"Well, we certainly owe you a lot more than a couple of cinnamon buns, Abe. You were a true friend when we needed you."

"So, how's Tilly getting along? I know it's been real tough on her. I didn't really want to ask her, bein' a man and all."

"Actually, Abe, Tilly is quite remarkable. She sure handled it a lot better than me, what with the surgery and all. I thought she'd be down for some time," said Charlie as he fought back a tear.

"You know, Charlie, ole' Doc there and his wife, they sure did the best they could under the circumstances."

Abe gestured towards the barn where Barney and Jim stood looking over the fence towards the house.

"But, ya know what I think, Charlie? I think the real heroes that day were those two boys of yours over there by the barn."

"Not a doubt in my mind, Abe."

From inside the house once again came the sound of Tilly's voice. "Hey, you two. Are you men coming in or not? The coffee and rolls are getting cold. Come on now. I've got a baby that needs a diaper and feeding. "

"We better go in, Abe. Maybe Tilly will let you hold the baby when she's been fed. Who knows? Maybe she'll even like old bearded geezers even like you."

Charlie and Abe stood to go into the kitchen and waived to Doctor Andersen's buggy as it clipped-clopped past the house. Out in the pasture the cattle were mooing and Suzy knew it would soon be time for her to bring them in to the barn. Somewhere came the crowing of a rooster and over by the pig sty the squeals of a new litter of piglets could be heard. Barney and Jim? Well, sensing that all seemed well once again, they just shook their heads, snorted, then quietly plodded off towards the shade of the grove of trees down behind the barn.


## The End

About this story. My grandparents, Ford and Luella Lincoln lived on a farm in Hinton Township north of Lakeview. Their only child, my father, Charles Lincoln, was born during a late winter storm in March. Doctor Kelsey, for whom our local hospital is named, was snowed in there for three days. They also had a team of draft horses named…you guessed it…Barney and Jim.

Dallas Ford Lincoln Copyright 2017

Made in the USA
Columbia, SC
07 August 2017